To Have To Follow

Julie Maclean & Terry Quinn

Indigo Dreams Publishing

First Edition: To Have To Follow
First published in Great Britain in 2016 by:
Indigo Dreams Publishing Ltd
24 Forest Houses
Halwill
Beaworthy
EX21 5UU
www.indigodreams.co.uk

Julie Maclean & Terry Quinn have asserted their right under the Copyright, Designs and Patents Act 1988 to be identified as the authors of this work.
©2016 Julie Maclean & Terry Quinn

ISBN 978-1-910834-14-5

British Library Cataloguing in Publication Data. A CIP record for this book can be obtained from the British Library.

This book is sold subject to the condition that it shall not, by way of trade or otherwise, be lent, re-sold, hired out, or otherwise circulated without the author's and publisher's prior consent in any form of binding or cover other than that in which it is published and without a similar condition including this condition being imposed on the subsequent purchaser.

Designed and typeset in Palatino Linotype by Indigo Dreams.
Printed and bound in Great Britain by 4Edge Ltd
www.4edge.co.uk

Cover design by Ronnie Goodyer from an idea by the authors.

Papers used by Indigo Dreams are recyclable products made from wood grown in sustainable forests following the guidance of the Forest Stewardship Council.

Foreword

As joint winners of the inaugural Geoff Stevens Memorial Poetry Prize our collections were published by Indigo Dreams Publishing in 2013.

Winning that prize and launching our books together in the Black Country that same year put us on the same page. We come from similar worlds; both born in England in the fifties and both travellers and poetry lovers.

We continued writing to each other, sharing ideas about poetry, publishing and the weather. This seemed important with the world between us – one writing from the north of England and the other from the Antipodes.

In December 2014 we decided to start using each other's poems as triggers. This project is the product of a year's work, born of that original poetry prize. Gratitude and thanks go to Ronnie Goodyer and Dawn Bauling of Indigo Dreams.

Terry and Julie, January 2016

Acknowledgements

Poems in this collection have appeared in *The North, Ink Sweat and Tears 12 Days of Christmas, Cordite Poetry Review, The Emma Press* anthology *'The Sea,' Australian Poetry Journal*. Thank you to the editors.

Previous publications

Julie Maclean
Kiss of the Viking, Poetry Salzburg, 2014
When I saw Jimi, Indigo Dreams Publishing, 2013

Terry Quinn
The Amen of Knowledge, Indigo Dreams Publishing, 2013
away, Poetry Monthly Press, 2010

CONTENTS

When Temporal Lobes	Maclean	5
On January 3rd	Quinn	6
Rasputin	Maclean	7
Wakes	Quinn	8
Camino	Maclean	9
The Coral Island	Quinn	11
Caseus Magnus – Big Cheese	Maclean	12
On not being there	Quinn	13
Far From	Maclean	14
Rules of Detection	Quinn	15
Walking with Joan Didion in Central Park	Maclean	16
Statement of Accounts	Quinn	17
Garuda	Maclean	19
The Seven Seas	Quinn	20
Something in the Eyre	Maclean	23
The End of the Ice Age	Quinn	24
Diva	Maclean	26
Alice is over there	Quinn	27
Brief Encounter Poet to Poet	Maclean	28
Day Trip to Bristol	Quinn	29
Emily Dickinson as an Octopus with a Pre-death Plan	Maclean	31
that New Idea	Quinn	32
Stonehenge in the Ley of the Dark	Maclean	33
Curious	Quinn	34

When Temporal Lobes

ignite like Christmas lights
down High Street

she is upright in a bentwood chair
/resin replica/

can't see or hear
not a sound

normally susceptible to suspense
/can't seem to shake it/

never expecting a good thing
to come of it

the crate of her skull
a pulse of epiphanous bliss

she thinks in tongues
of a thousand angels Gabriel

couldn't imagine a suicide
bomber or serial killer

knows everything about us
some days she takes little walks

past hospital wards with white views
a clipped, aching feel about them   /to us/

carrying out her marvellous plan
over crumpled pages, musical scores

child of the cosmos
Jesus lives!   /for five minutes/

On January 3rd

I will pause
as I usually do
before cracking the hard cover
and checking whether my birthday
falls on a weekend
and then some random stuff
like how many cubic centimetres
equal a cubic inch
or the currency in Sweden

and so meander onto
a pure white page
which is of course
the first day of the year
which will remain blank
as will the second
except for the note
that will read

see previous year

which I hope will be annoying
when I want to check a fact
in decades ahead
when I'll curse myself
as I usually do
for not buying the damn thing
in mid December
before hibernation settles
like snow in impossible villages
on cards I will soon take down.
It's Kroner by the way.

Rasputin

He wrestles bears and blue-skinned girls with tattooed arms
where swallows in small skies are ringed in barbed wire
Gulag-style

And boys in crotch-huggers, pointy-toed slides in summer
fringes of blonde hair slashing their angel faces
in oblique angles

He brings bears to their knees   sickle cropping history
across tundra where philosophers moved mountains
and starved, now shale wells beam light to West windows

On his charger, up the railway track and back,
he gallops to brassy minarets, bad haircuts and leather jackets
from the Eighties

Baring his chest of rolled cheese, his biceps flick off mosquitoes,
reining in goose pimples, gypsies and whores
when the first snow thaws

Wakes

Smoke from excursions
would be shaping these fields
with whispers of summer
as girls in scarves
and boys with severe haircuts
would be getting close
to catch what might be true.

In today's paper there's a sketch
of what might pass for a view
lines of track
cutting through acres
of cheap souvenirs of the Tower
drilling deep into memories
of the Pathé News
those kids would have watched
where nodding donkeys
gushed black oil
over guys in overalls.

As the train slows
for Pleasure Beach station
I shake off the past and present
tense for the future
where those donkeys strike
under pressure
not daring to nod
with their hooves planted
in fields of gas
as solid as candy floss
bought by the boys and girls
in their week of summer.

Camino

Like a tramp or a pilgrim
it is my intent to walk
in this patch of quiet
to the last full stop,
dip into catacombs,
pre-pay my spot.

From Canterbury
I will ensure my laptop
is backed up
against all disaster
like lightning
or a heat wave,
though I am travelling
at the end of season when
stable conditions
are expected.

It is some distance from
home when I ask myself
what I am doing here
with blisters and cracking knees.

It's not the easy route, I know
like that party when I found myself
kissing another man on your bed
or dashing to the Antipodes
to avoid being married.
I want to stretch something.

But in this enforced solitude
I find torn souls from last century,
cairns dedicated not to explorers
but to ballistics that exploded the lives
of ordinary loving others.

And when I call to
tell you I have reached
St Bernard's Pass
a thousand feet up,
a million miles from
Wimbledon
you ask me if I am near a TV.

Me, in the five-star
luxury position
of gaining repentance
and above all, forgiveness.

Instead, I find myself
back in the emptiness,
a barking frog
that nobody can hear,
especially you,
with the hangover from hell,
everything stretched to snapping.

The Coral Island

Somewhere in the Java Sea
roughly the size of Sark
with a Lookout Hill
views of smooth beaches
falls of fresh water
forests and pineapples
a call to adventure

Ballantyne's book
unfurled after fifty years
but ready aye ready

were there coves
was the temperature
a steady twenty three degrees

no snakes (touch wood)
no sea creatures that sting
which is a reminder
to check for a medicine chest
with plasters and Ventolin

reading glasses
wide brimmed hat
and a sort of large cushion
that could double as a mattress
and talking of doubling up

but that's getting ahead
let's get past the colour plate
to the first chapter

*Roving has always been
and still is my ruling passion*

Caseus Magnus – Big Cheese

I have sometimes wondered
what people see in the moon.
Nearing a full one
I feel the pull and want to howl
in its general direction

but have never been tempted
to stake a claim
by the Sea That Has Become Known
/in spite of its Latin name/
or make love in the Sea of Fecundity,
though how that occurs remains a mystery.
The Sea of Nectar, on the other hand
sounds like pure scam.

Why would I want to swap my swivel chair
for a side dark or near
when neither comes close to The Beach Café
where pancakes are to die for
or my backyard where mudlarks
and lorikeets keep me amused all day
padding about terra firma
with its endless supply of moth
and proper nectar

When after dark and I am alone
in the room with the heater off or on
stuck for words I'm drawn
to the clack-clack of frogs and find myself
chasing the tilting face of a hare
behind the veil of a place
made rare and beautiful by the plain sailing fact
/wholly underestimated/ of *not* being there

On not being there

but being here
in the local Odeon
watching Casablanca
at midday on a Monday

and I am alone

as crowds jostle in suspect bazaars
while Laszlo orders a brandy
and Louis lights another cigarette
from a flame that glows white
on black seats in an empty cinema

just a thousand, Rick
you'll get it back
an exit visa for Lisbon
New York or Rio

not February in Preston again
with the heater on in a pleasant home
checking the What's On
for unexpected diversions

always that bit short
of being there.

Far From

I was happy in crowds until I met you,
Man in Nest above the Bullring,
Lama praying in a cave
but now I want
the nearest neighbour
down a dirt track miles from town
red gum flowering.

I won't care if my wall of quiet
is fisted by the sound of
an indeterminate engine
because there will be one
but it won't get through
and I won't need to hide behind
the slatted pine where passion fruit
is dropped by a greedy parrot.

For all they say
I won't be lonely in my life less shared,
but invigorated not showering every day
and making up lies
should a stranger appear
expecting the door
to be opened   It won't be

and when it turns chilly
I am in my hut on McMurdo,
gorging from the belly of a seal
no manners at all
in this exquisite laboratory
where the only chatter is mine,
thanking some god for the physics
in hot buttered toast, a cup of tea.

The Rules of Detection

Who
was in the café at Borders
sneakily reading about the five W's
before slipping the book back
in time for the midday train
checking St Martin's clock and

What
the bloody hell is that
half way up the Rotunda and

When
did it click
that bookshops are wonderful
and so are notebooks
1142/May 23/2005/man's head/
5W: Rule 1/ flyer/
Benjamin Verdonck/performance artist and

Where
did he find the twigs
to build a ten foot nest
on the side of a building
two hundred feet above ground
in the centre of Birmingham and

Why
is this art
why now why here
but most of all
why is no one bothered that
There Is A Man
In A Nest
Above The Bullring

Walking with Joan Didion in Central Park

You have to be there early spring
to catch the pastel knit
dipping under a cherry bomb
of Yoshino and Kwanzan
veering north to Harlem Meer
feeling nothing but disappointment
at the lake from a terrace of tourists
longing for a flint of sapphire
to pluck her Sacramento gaze
from the drear of artificial waterways

> Armoured in a meteor of bangs
> she shifts through ragged spans
> of Manhattan schist happy to return
> to the Angel of the Waters
> seen from the shadow
> of the aqueduct stretching
> and flexing her wings
> hoping for a meeting with lost ones
> knowing full well wax melts

She stops to touch
sometimes to listen
to what Rat the granite
boulder has to say
Sole original matter
in this rectangle
of manufactured green
he can be heard
Glacial erratic, curious bird,
she picks over murdered girls,
a hermit in a man-made cave,
rape-beats of boys and mariners
Walking with Didion – my special fiction

Statement of Accounts

On the occasion of receiving
a handwritten envelope
it's saved till last
like getting rid of the broccoli
before the tasty stuff
though that's changed recently

but be that as it may
there's one this morning
resting between junk mail
and this official looking thing
from a department store
I dealt with years ago.

I have an opening balance of nothing
I haven't earned any points
I have a new balance of nothing

I am also required to pay
a minimum payment of nothing
by a non-specified date.

This is excellent stuff
and there's more overleaf
such as an annual interest rate of 26.478%
on any standard rate purchase
that I've never made

and here's the best bit
there is a £12 late payment fee
on the applicable amount of nothing
and a number to call at 5p a minute

I suppose I'll have to do something
but now it's time for the treat

and without going into detail
one of my oldest friends
has written to tell me about
the water colour he's just started
ordering a conservatory
learning Japanese
the beautiful woman
that's now sharing his life
and their trip to Manhattan

and I'm pleased for him
really I am
and I will reply
after I've figured out
what to do about nothing.

Garuda

At the end, once I'd arrived, swallow from the south,
I barely recognised my bird father. It was his pecked look.

The ribs of his cage beat a hymn rhythm on his heart.

It wouldn't stop, like some wind-up toy you tire of,
like the long-time sick and dying.

His djembe throat drummed on while I sat and held his
featherless wing.

At Wolf Hour I found him perched on the branch
of his nest-bed looking out to an orchestra.

/Night clouds always seem remote, in a hurry to leave the night
behind but they stopped, parted curtains for his entertainment/

How kind that March moon, spotlight on jazz and swing,
his love of that, not drama so much.

As I stood in the doorway of that requiem he told his last joke.

Then I could understand why she kept the honeymoon on her
bedside table.
Black and white, he made a sonata in a check shirt.
Walnut pipe at a jaunty angle where a flute would sit,
then a clarinet.

When nurses came to dress that sparrow body in a shroud
he saw his own reflection in the wardrobe mirror sky and was
afraid.

The stench of breath from the lair of wolves would sap the song
of any bird
but his mouth turned sweet as the breath flew out.

Later he returned, lingering in a tree, his nest of gold spanning seven continents, eighty countries.

But the morning chorus failed to wake the day. A robin tapped at the window. A squirrel scrabbled among ash under the miserable pine.

The Seven Seas

This shouldn't be difficult
North, Irish, Black,
and I'm just relaxing
as the problem of the Atlantic
springs to mind

I open my mouth
just a bit wider
should I move my tongue
or leave it like Italy
dipping into the Med
that's another

I'm moved to squint
into a ruthless sun
trying not to make sense
of shanties drifting
lower left one occlusal
upper right two palatal
something about a buccaneer
and pieces of seven on Treasure Island
lost in the Caribbean

this is a fine way
to daydream an afternoon away
maybe next time
the order of the Planets
or the Periodic Table

there's a brief surge of pride
in the skills I've gained
over the last few years
to avoid reality
before

I start to think
about forthcoming negotiations
regarding scale and polish
where my chances are as slim
as an Arctic iceberg in the Indian Ocean
which doesn't really help
as an ocean isn't a sea, is it.

Something in the Eyre

it is day twelve and I'm worn
as the gibber

on this saline plain
when an arrow of moonstone

shot from an ocean of quartz
pierces my snow-blind eye

pristine crystal sets a shoal of marlin
leaping into the sun as far as we can see

a giant eel heaves itself
from the core of this artesian heart

its scoria body encrusted with salt diamonds
folds of leather moist to the touch

from the seep of feeling springs
there to remind me

while roots of salt bush suck the last drop
as an illusion spreads its ice blanket over us

The End of the Ice Age

was not at five past three
on a Thursday in late September
though to be fair
what the boy was actually saying
with some enthusiasm
was the glaciers stopped here
ten thousand years ago

the girl was waving her arms
(I can recognize exasperation)
don't be a nerd
look at the views
which was what I'd been doing
so I was on her side

but he wasn't giving up
this is millstone grit
before the Ice Age this was a sea
just imagine fish floating
along this very path
so I did
and I was on his side

she waved her arms again
where's your romance
he said science is beautiful
and they hardly noticed me
which was also beautiful
as they carried on up to the tarn

and I carried on back
to the Roaches Tea Room
where Anna would be waiting
wondering whether to ask
did she think of me

as a man of romance or science
but settled on asking
did she want tea or cappuccino.

Diva

When I staged *Alice* in a school room closer to Antarctica
than Bristol –
rabbit hole a patch of industrial carpet
where a table leg chafed,
I thought I was headed for Broadway.

Ha! Not in the eyes of the class of '87.
Relegated to voyeur with minimalist intervention
my sole responsibility – jungle sounds
Alice on quasi safari in the spotlight
reading *Fractured Fairytales*
Rock Lobster for the bong scene. I don't know why.

Entire play so professional without me –
so fishy, so rabbity,
so brilliant baby-throwing, mad-arsed right.

Yes! I had a red hot hand of super-sized playing cards,
same-sex crustacean and a bonkers queen   hair band
holding it all together,

                            but when I looked in the mirror,
my marriage had foundered on a papier-mâché thing,
besmirched by surreal doings in the bio box
with someone suntanned and dumb.

It wasn't long before I was drowning
in that fat Southern Ocean of Tears.
Bastard cat grinning from a cardboard gum tree
ear to ear in Act III.

Alice is over there

Said the woman with a white badge
pointing to row upon row of Wonderland
where some books were short and fat
some long and thin
some looked heavy some looked fun
and one was all of those things

"This isn't right," exclaimed the Customer
"There's only one Alice"

"That is not so" said Alice in a pink dress
"She's correct" said Alice in a hat
which set off a deafening chorus
of girls' voices that right had been left
but they were not, absolutely not,
some kind of cheap copy
except for a slim volume on the top shelf
who proudly bristled that that's exactly what she was
until an old hardback demanded SILENCE then exclaimed
"Do not choose them, I am the original Alice,
these are copywrongs,
so you may pick me as it is my anniversary"
which caused a huge fluttering

"That's quite enough, Sir," said the Assistant firmly
"we've all been Alice since 1907, so please leave."

she fussed around the shelves calming them all down
muttering to herself about consequences
before disappearing down a corridor marked
To Science and Natural History.

Brief Encounter Poet to Poet

When you arrive
  on the 9.30 from the north
    you seem upset
      by slave chains in wait
        on city walls near the Nails
          and shrapnel
            pitting the sandstone
              of Chatterton's St Mary's

              I'm sorry you refuse
              the last few steps
              to the top of the Wills Tower
              for fear of meeting your maker
              or stepping on a dead pigeon

                    so I go up alone
                    and when we get
                    to the museum
                    Mobile Lovers
                    have arrived
                    checking their phones
                    but you ignore them
                    in favour
                    of the mono-plane
                    aimed at the Arctic

            We go looking for a cardigan
            one with a pocket for a pencil
            and Moleskine notebook
            to record what's left of our
            train-ticket lives

        When you're gone
      I'm half-strength coffee
    in the white space called Arnolfini
    all hardbacks and shadows,
  cash register with no ring,
white noise deafening

Day Trip to Bristol

You were right.

In the time it took
for that awful cake
in that bland gallery
we could have been walking
taking notes to spray its walls
with lines of your youth

like Banksy
just up the hill
on bricks of streets
of offices you'd hated

to the tower
where you raced
keen wind
up stone rigging
to the edge of distance
watching for topsails
of clippers
bearing south before you

while down below
a bell stays silent
a bloody big bell
so it's mind the steps
and mind the ropes

hitched to a city
that tried to hold you
tied to quays
where sugar sweetened the Squares
and we know what that meant

but here and now
to risk touching rope
just for the feel of casting off
waving goodbye
with a ribbon borrowed
from those Morris Dancers.

Emily Dickinson as an Octopus with a Pre-Death Plan

I
From this high-care low-life facility where my head lolls
in the briny bowl Doctor Death asks what my priorities are
What goals I have in the short term
What I am prepared to sacrifice   What not   I want
to make bad choices   pick a fight, drink more wine,
raid the fridge at midnight, steal those earrings, disembowel
carnations, rip to shreds that New Idea then shoot for a wave
where an octopus looks me in the eye like a Hindu god
with the wisdom of a new-born babe, takes my measure,
shows me personality, holds a tea party with nothing in it
but chocolate cake and opioids then hides me in her cave –
two of us minus our ancestral shells sharing a spliff,
smoking our guffawing heads off

II
Back in the tank outside visiting hours we are chastened
and when nobody's looking she oozes across to greet me in
redness of excitement   I touch her head,
she turns creamy white, relaxed like no one I know,
so many lobes coiled around her throat meet my mind
She spits salt water in my face to show me how much
she knows me, she knows me, knows me, bored to death by
melancholia she squeezes her boneless body through aquarium
bars – it's mayhem across that Amherst lawn suckering
everything in her path – down down down to the water,
changing colour, texture, spots, commas – slashing pages with
short lines – long-necked funny unlived Em playing with rage
and form, dying tired without me – alone

that New Idea

came to me
while I was texting you
from a bench at Kent's Bank

but you know how it is
new phone
predictive textile

I wanted to tell you
I'd recognized a Copper Beech
and the next thing is
a Morecambe Bay breeze
had the branches bending
and straightening
bending and straightening

textiles bending and
sine waves breaking on
shores of smooth grey bark

wind panels bending
turning a rotor
in some sort of circuit
that's tied to the branch
(that bit's a bit hazy)
and micro-amps tapped
we could call it sapped

somewhere down the trunk
by the bloke in a panama
who's been staring at me
for the last few minutes
from his front garden.

Stonehenge in the Ley of the Dark

From under an old army blanket
we watched the sun rise over Friars Heel
before high wire and solstice porn ruined our Druid fantasy.
We startled every kissing gate after elderberry picking,
a flask of tea and an argument over a short skirt.

And now,
hem grown long without you,
I can't stop searching
for a marking stone
or tump of trees
on a mound by the weir
to show me the dead-true way
to a sighted track
where the knapper traded
flint and salt,
and a boulder shaped for a man's back
splayed in sacrifice
was shot by rays on a Midsummer
slaughtering day in a Malvern cave.

So many times I lay upon that sarsen stone
as Tess in full view of the moon's opinion
desperate to find the beckoning fire on the hill,
only now realising that if I could have
been still, under the bend of that copper lea,
understanding how a grove of beech is light
because it has no light
roots wrapped quiet, curious but clenched for dear or sour life,
that light would have aligned me with the boy
who drowned in the lake,
marked by an oak bench and marigolds.

Curious

I like to think
that walking these lines
will take me to unexpected places
a hidden track
Stonehenge by moonlight
the finding of a tump

and it does and I'm happy
though you may get to thinking
that it's not quite enough

and you'd be right
especially if you'd been in Shrewsbury
the day before yesterday
and a slightly open door
to that medieval house
and the tension as I realised
without a shadow of doubt
that she was going in
and I was going to have to follow

not for the first time
and not for the first time
her daft excuse worked
as we left with the owner's smile
and history of a hallway table

which we talked about over tea
on an oak bench by the river
where she stumped me
by adding a question
regarding our future
which I haven't thought about
and is hard to imagine.